Poksy's Party

Annette Claire Wilson

AuthorHouse™
1663 Liberty Drive
Bloomington, IN 47403
www.authorhouse.com
Phone: 1 (800) 839-8640

Published by AuthorHouse 03/05/2015

ISBN: 978-1-4969-6782-4 (sc)
ISBN: 978-1-4969-6790-9 (e)

Library of Congress Control Number: 2015901687

Print information available on the last page.

authorHOUSE®

To all the children I had the opportunity to spend time with and grow with.

I learned a whole new life being with you:

Adam, Elon, Lois, Andie, Allon, Sarah, Shirley, Ricky, Matt, Chris, Torrie, Jesse, Anna, Pet, Gaius, Shem, Damie, May, Rose, Joe, Hezron, and Jonah.

Special thanks to Vernette for giving Poksy his dimples.

Poksy was born with two dimples, one on each side of his face. When he was born, he had the loudest cry; the nurses came to check on him and his mom and were delighted to see his dimples as he cried. When he gave a wink, the dimples appeared as well; the nurse poked her little finger in his dimple, and from then on, she called him Poksy, and so did all the other nurses. Poksy became his nickname.

When Poksy was just about turning six years old, at the end of winter his mother was planning a major clean-up of all the storage boxes of toys, books, and crafts that he had grown out of.

Poksy never wanted to get rid of anything, but he promised his mother that he would help her clean out the boxes. Poksy did not really like cleaning, but he thought if he was around while his mother was cleaning out the boxes, he could keep some things she wanted to throw out. Poksy was sentimental about everything he owned, even the waste paper; he had an excuse for keeping everything his mother thought was necessary to throw away or give to someone in need.

There was a box in the storage room with drawings of sailboats and flags all over it. Poksy was curious and wanted to open the box and see what was in it; he asked his mother for permission to open the box, and she granted him permission to open the box.

3

Poksy quickly opened the box and poured out everything on the floor. He went through the papers, books, and toys; there was a bag with birthday cards from Poksy's first, second, third, fourth, and fifth birthday, and some craft work that his father had saved from Poksy's first grade class. His father thought that his work looked like the craftwork of a ten-year-old.

As Poksy looked through the papers and the birthday cards in the box, he asked, "Why do I have to wait so long to have another birthday party, Mom?"

His mother explained, "Birthdays only come once a year, Poksy. They're a celebration of the same date of the same month, but a different year; that's why the day isn't always the same."

"Mom, it just feels like it takes so long," Poksy persisted.

"Well, that's because we wait for the new school term in September to have your party."

Poksy nodded. His birthday was the first day of August, and since most people went away on vacation in August, it was better to have his party in September so that all his school friends could celebrate with him.

Poksy pulled out a card, looked at it, and said, "I can't even remember my first or second birthday, Mom. Not even my third!"

His mom smiled, rubbed him on the head, and asked, "What about the fourth?"

Poksy remembered his fourth birthday very well, because his Uncle Jeff made a special trip from Ohio. He brought Poksy's birthday cake; it was made in the shape of a truck and decorated with red and white icing all over, and black icing for the wheels of the truck.

When Uncle Jeff got to Poksy's home, he lifted Poksy up in the air, kissed him all over, rubbed his head (which Poksy loved), and promised to spend the best birthday with him.

At the time, he was eating popcorn from a bag, and when his uncle turned him around, almost half of the popcorn fell on the floor, making the shape of a circle.

Everyone thought that Poksy would cry, because he always cried when things spilled or fell, but he didn't.

Poksy thought it was the funniest sight. He laughed and laughed, and he had the loudest, happiest laugh.

"That was the best part of having a birthday party, even if it was not my real birthday. That was really fun, Mom!" Poksy said.

"I remember how happy you looked at that moment, Poksy," Mom replied.

Afterward, when everyone picked up the spilled popcorn, Poksy joined in to help and said, "Mom, Mom! Look, I did not cry, even if I lost half of my popcorn. Wow! Am I a big boy now, Mom? Uncle Jeff, look! I did not cry; I am a big boy now!"

Poksy was elated, bubbling with excitement, and had one of his best days.

Poksy sat on the floor and went through all the pictures and cards, reading them one at a time, and trying hard to recall events from the first, second, or third birthday, but he could not remember; he was disappointed that he could not remember those events, which seemed to be so much fun by looking at the pictures.

He said, "Boy, oh boy, how could I not remember such good times and fun? Look at these fun, cool pictures."

He wondered if every child was like him, unable to remember their past birthdays, and getting to know about them by looking at old pictures. Or was it just him that had such a problem?

He kept muttering, "How could a child forget something so fun, his own birthday party?"

The pictures were bright and colorful, and everyone looked happy. Poksy looked at a lot of pictures with his face covered with cake and ice cream and lots of sprinkles.

Poksy thought about his coming birthday and checked how many months he had to wait before his birthday.

It is a long way off, Poksy thought; three months is a long time.

He thought for a while and then said, "Mom, must we wait for all these months to have a birthday party?"

His mother reminded him that a birthday comes only once a year.

Poksy said he understood, but he thought it was unfair that one should have to wait all that time in order to have a party.

He thought for a while and said to himself, in a quiet voice, "Just a party; I think we should have a party now, and a real birthday party when September comes. I will call this party Poksy's Fun Day. I will invite all my friends; we'll have lots of fun and ice cream too. No gifts, just fun, fun, fun, good games, and lots of good treats."

Poksy got up from the floor and went to his mom and said that he would like to have a party more often, and not have to wait once a year.

Poksy's mom thought for a while and agreed that he should have a party more than once a year. She promised Poksy that she would mention this idea to his father when he came home from work.

Poksy was excited and waited for his dad, looking through the window. Meanwhile, he forgot all about the cards and pictures on the floor. He grew very quiet, wondering why his father was taking so long to get home, because he had something very important to tell him.

Poksy looked out the window at every car driving by, with his head moving, left-right, left-right, with no sight of his father. He felt that his father was taking forever. He had never had to wait for his father before, so it seemed longer than usual, and he was getting very, very impatient.

Poksy asked his mom to call his father and find out why he was taking so long to get home.

His mom assured him that his father was on time; she suggested that he find something to do to distract him from the waiting period.

Poksy agreed; he went into the kitchen but could not focus; every time he heard a car, he would run to the window to see if it was his father.

Poksy's mother suggested to him that while he was waiting for his father, they should decide which charitable organizations he would like to give his things to.

The town Poksy lived in had lots of children and lots of kid-friendly organizations, like Friendly Friends, Kids for Kids, Best Budz, and the Children Helping Children Club (CHCC).

Poksy loved the idea of helping children who were less fortunate than he was by giving and sharing things with them, but he thought it would be better to buy something new to give away, because he wanted to keep everything he had in the box. As you would imagine, his parents did not agree with that idea.

His mother decided to pack some of the clothing and toys in a box and allow Poksy to choose the books he had a special liking for, so that she could give away the rest of the books and clothing and toys.

Poksy did, but with a great deal of hesitation; once again, he started going through every book, and to him every book was special, because he wanted to read them over and over again.

When his father arrived home, Poksy was so busy that he did not hear the car pull up in the driveway; he didn't even hear when his father walked into the house.

Poksy went to the kitchen to ask his mother if he could have a jelly doughnut; he saw his father taking off his coat. He was so excited to see his father, he started jumping up and down.

"Dad, Dad!" Poksy exclaimed. "Guess what? I'm going to have a party with lots of friends, lots of snacks, and fun, fun, fun."

"Where did that idea came from, Poksy?" his dad asked. "It's not your birthday just yet."

"Dad, September is so far away," he said, "and I just want to have some fun with my friends. It's a long, long time to wait."

His father looked surprised and asked Mom what brought about that idea. They both went on to explain again, and Poksy's father agreed that a party away from his birthday was a wonderful idea.

Just then, Poksy's father asked, "May I make a suggestion?"

Poksy got a little nervous, thinking that his father was about to change something in his plan for the party.

That was far from the case.

Poksy's dad stood up and said, "I have a great idea. Let's have a neighborhood party for families and children who are less fortunate, and for all the children of the CHCC."

When Poksy heard that suggestion, he jumped out of his chair, ran toward his dad, and started shouting and jumping, saying, "Boy, oh boy, Dad! This is so cool, that's a great idea. Thanks, Dad, thanks, Mom; this is going to be really fun."

Poksy could not believe what he had just heard from his father.

Poksy said, "Boy, this is going to be real fun! Mom, can I call Elon to tell him?"

His mom said, "It is too late to call anyone now, you will have to wait until tomorrow."

Poksy's father said he would contact the CHCC, prepare the invitation for the neighborhood children, and find a place to hold the party, while his mother would take care of all the food, snacks, cakes, and drinks, and Poksy would choose the games, make a list of friends to invite, write out the invitations, and get the envelopes ready to be mailed.

Poksy was so excited he could not think straight. He could not settle down; he was bubbling with excitement and started asking his father lots and lots of questions. Poksy went and stood next to his dad and asked, "Dad, if I invite all of my friends, will we have enough room for everyone? Do you think I can invite all my school friends and my friends in Miss Ella's class too?"

Poksy could not stop, and he went on and on about the party. His dad thought for a while and said, "Sure, Poksy, all the children can come and have a good time with you."

"Boy, oh boy," Poksy said, jumping up and down as always whenever he was happy or excited.

His dad said he would ask a few parents from the club to help put things together with him. He said, "I want all the children to have fun, just as Poksy wished for; if all goes well, we can do this every year, maybe even encourage clubs in other towns to do the same for their kids."

Poksy's mom was also very excited about the party, and Poksy was elated to see how excited his mom and dad were.

"Honey, I love those ideas," Poksy's mom said to his dad.

His dad replied, "I am getting as excited as Poksy is. I caught myself saying 'Boy oh boy,' just like Poksy."

Poksy's mom called out, "Come over here, Poksy!"

Poksy came running; she opened her arms, caught Poksy, and said, "You, my little man, what a lovely way to give other children a chance to have a good time."

She gave Poksy a squeeze and a kiss on the cheek, rubbed his head, and poked him in his dimples. Poksy squealed with delight, loving every moment with his mom; he said softly, "Mom, I have a secret, do you want to hear it?

"Sure," she replied.

"Okay, bend over, Mom."

She did, and Poksy got close to her ear and whispered, "I love you, Mom, and Dad too."

"Oh Poksy, I know, and we do love you very, very much."

Poksy went into his favorite "Boy, oh boy" chant.

Poksy suddenly got very quiet.

His dad looked at him, gave him a rub on the head, and asked him where all his excitement and joy went.

Poksy asked what would happen when his birthday came; would he have a real birthday party?

His father assured him that he would have a special party on his birthday.

Poksy felt much better; all of a sudden, he got joyful and happy again.

Dinner was ready; it was one of Poksy's favorite meals: baked potatoes stuffed with broccoli and cheese, corn on the cob, baked chicken drumsticks, and string beans. Poksy slid down the stairs and said, "Boy, oh boy, I smell the best food, and I know what it is: baked potatoes and chicken, right, Mom?"

"How did you know, you little smarty? You have a good nose," said his mom.

"I can't wait to dig in," said his dad. "The house smells so good with your cooking, my dear; thanks for a great dinner."

"You're welcome, the pleasure is mine," his mom said with a smile.

As they sat at the dinner table, they talked about the children, the party, the games, the food, the fun everyone would have at that special event.

Poksy sat quietly for a while, thinking about the fun games, the cake, the ice cream, and all the treats there would be at the party; suddenly, he shouted, "We can play water balloons and jump in the bag." He was very good at that game. Each child would get in a bag, tied at the waist, and try jumping a long distance; whoever jumped the farthest, without falling, got a very big prize.

His mother said, "It would be nice to have a talent show for the kids. We could call it Show Off Your Talent, and the kids could come up and sing, tell a story, read a poem, perform a play, or build something with Lego."

"Great idea," Poksy said, "and I have a talent already."

Poksy's dad said, "I will ask Mr. Haynes to build us an outdoor stage, and you, my dear, with all the ladies from your book club and Mothers on the Go club, could decorate it and organize all the talent events."

Poksy's mom was very happy that he and his dad liked her idea.

Everyone in the neighborhood knew and loved Mrs. Planner; she belonged to several clubs in the community and knew everyone by name, so it was not a problem for her to call them up and get things going, as she always did.

Now they had to pick a day and time that would be good for everyone.

Poksy suggested the last Saturday in May, before families left for summer vacation.

His mother said if they shared the responsibilities among the community members, there would be no need to rush things, and they could have everything done on time. She was positive because she was used to doing things at the various clubs and was a good organizer. She always said, "I can get things done in the wink of an eye," and she always gave a wink.

Poksy's mom and dad agreed that the first thing to do was to choose the venue, get permission to build the outdoor stage, and send out the invitations; once they got those things out of the way, then everything else would fall into place nicely.

Poksy sat on the floor, writing the names of all his friends that he could remember.

His parents said that they would get to work on their plans in the morning.

"Oh my," Poksy's mom said suddenly. "Look at the time. I can't believe how late it is. It's way past bedtime for all of us."

She quickly got Poksy into bed and asked his dad to read him a very, very short story while she cleaned up the table and put things away. Poksy always loved his dad to read to him; he quickly jumped out of bed, grabbed a pile of books, spread them on the bed, and asked, "Dad, could you read this book, Brown Bear and the Sugar Bowl, please?"

Dad asked, "How long is this book, Poksy?"

"There are only fifteen pages," he replied.

"Remember, Mom said a short story," his dad replied. "Let's do this: I will read half of the story tonight, and if you wake up early, I can read the other half to you before I leave for work."

"Cool," Poksy replied.

He got under his cover, collected his soft teddy bears beside him, including his favorite brown and black bear, and said, "Now read slowly, Dad, I want Browny to hear the story too." That was what he named his little bear.

His dad started to read the story, while Poksy tried to stay awake. Poksy's favorite part of the story was when the bear got his head stuck in an old sugar bowl that the farmer left under a tree; just as Dad got to the paragraph, Poksy started to say the words together with his father: "And then the bear came and sniffed around and licked the rim of the bowl, put his nose inside the bowl, and then, he could not pull his head out."

Poksy started to laugh and said, "Dad, let's read this part again."

Dad replied, "Only one more time, Poksy, it's really late."

The next morning, Poksy got out of bed, rushed downstairs, and started to ask his mom about the party. She told him to hurry so that he would not be late for the school bus. Poksy rushed upstairs, brushed his teeth, washed his face, got dressed, and came downstairs again.

18

He asked, "What's for breakfast, Mom? Are you going to shop for the party today?" The words were just rumbling out of Poksy's mouth.

"Slow down, Poksy, sit down, and while we have breakfast, I will tell you my plans for today." She made pancakes and scrambled eggs for breakfast; as she served Poksy, she said, "I will call all my friends at my book club and tell them about your party. They can help us plan for your very special fun day, how about that? And I'm sure to have some good news for you when you get home from school. Now your bus will be here soon, you need to eat."

"Awesome," Poksy said.

"I think I hear your bus, let's go outside, Poksy."

Poksy picked up his backpack and ran out the door, with his mom right behind him.

"Oh, yes, Mom, it's the bus; it's right next to Jerry's house," Poksy said. "It will be here any moment now."

The bus pulled up in front of Poksy's house; Poksy got on, greeted the bus driver, and got into his seat next to the window. His mom waved good-bye and said, "Have a nice day at school."

Poksy waved back and shouted, "Thanks, Mom. I will tell my friends all about the party, okay? I love you, Mom. Good-bye!"

As the bus driver shut the door and slowly drove off, Poksy started to tell the children all about the party.

While Poksy was at school, his mom got her phone, notebook, and pen together and wrote down everyone she planned to call from her book club.

She then called Mrs. Getty, who always knew everything that was going on in the community. "Hello, Mrs. Getty," she said. "We're planning a big party for Poksy; do you know anyplace that can hold about a hundred people?"

"Wow, what kind of party is that?" Mrs. Getty asked. "One hundred people, that sounds like a ball dance or a wedding, but Poksy is too young for that. What's going on? Well, the only place I know is the small soccer field, right next to the river. Mr. Givens is in charge of that place; I can give you his number if you need it."

"Okay, great," Mrs. Planner said. "Can we set up a meeting later this week so that you and the other girls can help me with the party?"

"Oh sure, how about Thursday? That's a slow day for me," she replied.

"Let me give the other girls the day and see if it works for them all. I'll get back to you soon."

Poksy's mom thought that was a great idea. She called Mr. Givens right away.

When Poksy got home from school, he just dropped his backpack on the floor and asked, "Mom, are your friends going to help? Did you speak with anyone today? Am I going to have my fun day party?"

"Yes, you will have a party," Poksy's mom said. "Why don't you tell me about your day at school today?"

"Oh, I got an A on four of my papers, one B, one happy smiley face sticker, and one star. I color really, really well, my teacher said. Now tell me, am I going to have the party? My friends on the bus all want to come, but I could not tell them what day. I just said it would be really, really soon. Tell me when, Mom, please."

Poksy's Party

"Okay, Poksy, I did very well today. I spoke with my book club friends and called Mrs. Getty, who gave me the number for Mr. Givens, the community hall director. I explained to him why we need the field."

"What did Mr. Givens say?" Poksy asked.

"He said, 'Mrs. Planner, I love the idea. That is the best news I've heard all year,'" his mom said. "Poksy, he was almost as excited as you are, I am sure I heard him saying, 'Boy, oh boy.'"

Poksy giggled and then said, "Boy, oh boy, oh boy!"

"Mr. Givens asked me when we needed the field for, how many people we were going to have, what time we will start and finish, and what would we need from him. Before I could say anything, he offered to let us use the benches, tables, umbrellas, water coolers, and all the balls and games he had in the community storage.

"He said to me, 'I always wanted to do something for the kids in the community but never got around to doing so. This is so great, what your family is doing.' I told him this was all your idea, to have a fun day away from a birthday party, because you find it's hard waiting a whole year for a party."

Poksy was very, very happy and said, "Wow, Mom! That's great."

"Yes, Poksy, Mr. Givens was wonderful. I made a lot of progress with that one call."

Poksy grinned, and his two dimples showed on his face. "What's progress, Mom?"

"It means that I set up steps toward our goal, which is the party day of fun. I started the steps and completed a lot of them."

"Oh," said Poksy. "I hope Dad made progress too."

His mom laughed. "I'm sure he did; we'll find out when he gets home."

"How soon will he get home?"

"Soon enough," his mother said firmly.

"Can we call him and tell him all this?"

"Go and play," she replied, "and your father will be home before you know it. When he gets home, you can tell him everything."

Meanwhile, Poksy's dad spoke to a few of his colleagues about the community event, and they had lots of ideas to add to his plans.

Mark, the accountant in his office, said, "That's a very good idea; it sounds like you are having a carnival. Why don't you print tee shirts with the community building and some kids on them and give every child a tee shirt to wear on that day? The girls can wear a different color from the boys."

"Now that's interesting," Poksy's dad said. "I think I'll take you up on this idea."

Poksy's dad could not wait to get home to tell Poksy and his mom about his day at the office.

"Hello, hello, I'm home, where is everyone? I have some good news for you."

Poksy and his mom came racing out of the kitchen.

Poksy shouted, "We have good news too, Dad. I told all my friends on the bus today, and Mom spoke to Mr., Mr., ah, I forgot his name. Mom, what did you say his name was?"

"His name is Mr. Givens," Mom said.

"Oh yes, Mr. Givens. Mom, can you tell Dad what Mr. Givens said?"

Well, it really became a community event; everyone who knew about the party had an idea to offer. The plan went from a three-hour party to a whole day event. From simple games, to talent shows of every sort, Lego building, cup stacking, singing, fastest and slowest runners, rope jumping, juggling, throwing water balloons, and apple bobbing: every parent had a game in mind and an idea for fun.

Poksy's parents agreed that since it was a community event, as long as the games were wholesome and fun, they would not turn away any parent with a good idea, so the list of fun games kept growing.

One day, Poksy's dad brought home the invitations, and the family was very excited to look at them:

YOU ARE INVITED TO OUR FUN COMMUNITY PARTY.

AT

THE RIVERSIDE SOCCER FIELD

TIME: From 10 a.m. to 6 p.m.

June 1, 2013

Bring your swimsuit, your towel, your appetite, your smile, and your talent.

Breakfast, lunch, snacks, and dinner will be served.

When Poksy read the invitation he asked why anyone should bring their swimsuit, when there was no swimming pool.

His dad quickly reminded him about the water balloons and water slide games.

It did not require much of anything to get Poksy excited. He told his father that he had forgotten all about the water games.

Poksy thought that he would get some balloons and practice so that he could be the best balloon thrower of the boys when they come together.

The invitations were mailed out.

Poksy's dad, his uncle, the Givens, Morris, Bell, and Warner families got everything needed for the games.

Mrs. Planner and her book club friends got all the food, snacks, and drinks organized.

A few restaurants and pizza shops donated large amounts of food, and every family was asked to bring a dish of their choice.

As the days went by, the families got the invitations in their mailboxes.

The children were very excited to read about Poksy's event but could not understand why it was being held, because it was not a holiday or a birthday, so as soon as Poksy got on the bus next morning, Elon, his best friend, said, "Poksy, why are you having a party? It's not even your birthday."

Then the children started singing, "Poksy's having a party, Poksy's having a party." Leeann said in a sad tone, "A party with no birthday, you will not have any cake, no presents, and no glitter; that's no fun. Why do you want a party now, Poksy?"

Poksy said, "That's my idea, I want to have a party with no birthday, then I don't have to wait for a very, very, long time to have lots of fun. It's boring having to wait so long for my birthday."

The bus driver looked in his rear mirror and realized some of the children were not sitting in their seats. He said in a loud voice, "You know the rules, please stay in your seats, thank you."

They all answered in a slow tone, "Yes, Mr. Charles," and quietly sat down, remaining in their seats until they got to school. They continued with their chatter about the party.

Soon there was a buzz; everyone knew about the party and could not wait for the big event.

Two days before the party, Poksy's dad said, "Poksy, the mayor and the city clerk heard of the party and offered to donate reading books and candy to all the kids, and writing pens and pads to the adults as a way of showing gratitude for the community effort."

As the day drew closer, everyone got more excited at school; during break time and lunch time, Poksy's friends were busy talking about the party.

One child came up to Poksy and asked, "Why are you having a party now, Poksy, did you change your birthday?"

Someone else asked, "Will you have your real birthday party in September?"

Poksy was a little overwhelmed, having to answer all the questions about the party; he said, "I just want to have fun every day, and my birthday takes a long time to come, that's all, and you get to have fun with me too."

At that moment, the bell rang; they all had a big smile on their faces and finally understood Poksy; they rushed into class before the second bell rang.

Poksy's mom was reading the list of things to his dad about their idea of putting together fancy goody bags, with things like glow-in-the-dark rubber balls, candies, bubble bottles, playing cards, and miniature flashlights. Poksy was playing with his truck when he heard his mom mention a flashlight; he ran up to her and said, "Oh boy, I'd love to have a flashlight when I build my fort; will I get one, Mom?"

"Yes, Poksy, you will."

"That's cool," he said as his mom continued reading out the list to his dad; there were also fancy pencils and erasers that every family could take at the end of the party.

"Smart idea," said Poksy's dad.

The parents welcomed the idea and assigned a group of children to organize the filling of the bags two days before the party. The children came to Poksy's home after school to fill the bags. They got very excited; after Poksy's mom brought out the big bags of goodies, Jackie said, "Wow!"

"That's a lot of stuff," said John.

Poksy opened his eyes wide and pointed at the bags. "Mom, where did you have all of that?" he asked. "I never saw any of those things. Boy, oh boy, what cool stuff we have; it feels like the party already."

The children rushed to sit at the table and started to pile up stacks of their goodies, laughing, giggling, and chattering.

"Poksy, you have some real cool stuff", Mikey said.

"Oh yes, I like the little bubble bottle," said Luella, laughing, and she squeezed the bottle; the sudsy water sprayed on all of them at the table, and they all started laughing and giggling.

"Okay, have fun," Poksy's mom called from the kitchen, "but do not waste it; we want to make sure we have enough to fill all the bags."

The days leading up to the event were very busy; everyone in the neighborhood had something to do regarding the party. The stage was built, and buckets, drums, baskets, and bins were placed along the field. Lines were drawn and marked for running. The tables were set up, and some chairs were pulled out of storage, as well as all the games that could be found.

The men were in charge of all the drinks, ice, and sports. They worked hard at putting every known sport to the test.

The kids were told that the grounds should be kept clean; anything seen on the ground should be picked up and placed in the bins.

The night before the party, Poksy could not sleep; he was restless in his bed. All he could think about was the party: the water balloons, running around, and playing with his friends. At one time, he said aloud, "I want to sleep but I can't; the party won't let me."

His uncle told him one time, "Poksy, when you can't fall asleep, count sheep backwards; start from 30, that's a good number. Before you know it, you will be waking up in the morning."

It worked for Poksy in the past, but not this time; he just could not fall asleep. Poksy said to himself, "I wonder if Elon, Jackie, Luella, John, and Allon are asleep. I wonder if they are thinking about my party; maybe I can call them. Oh no, maybe they are asleep and their parents will pick up the phone."

Poksy was almost in tears; he got up and went to his parents' room and got into their bed. He said to them, "Mom, Dad, I can't fall asleep, I keep thinking about the party, and it just won't go away."

"It's okay," his dad said. "Stay here, and I'll carry you to your room when you fall asleep."

The day of the party finally arrived; all the kids were just waiting to dash out of their house to the playing field. They were shouting each other's names: "John, come on! Let's go and look for Ezra."

One of the boys shouted, "Let's get Jason, Ben, and Hezron; hurry, let's go!"

May, Lois, Damie, and Deland were all singing, "It's Poksy's party, let's go! Let's go!"

"We will have lots and lots of fun today," said Torrie.

As the families got closer to the field, they heard music, but did not know exactly where the music was coming from. To everyone's surprise, the high school band and a few musicians from the community were playing a special song they wrote for Poksy's party. They were on stage and entertained the community. When the crowd saw Mr. and Mrs. Planner coming from a distance, they all cheered and thanked Poksy's family for such a wonderful idea; the musicians went up to them and thanked them for inviting them to the party.

There was one big surprise: Someone made a cake just for Poksy.

The icing on the cake read: THANK YOU POKSY. GOOD IDEA. SEE YOU SAME DATE NEXT YEAR!

THE DAILY NEW

LOCAL BOY'S PARTY FOR

There was lots and lots of fun, good food, and people who lived in the community. They all got to know each other better.

The parents and community leaders took lots of pictures, and the television and media crew were present.

Poksy got his picture on the front page of the local newspaper; the article's headline was "POKSY'S PARTY, AND A COMMUNITY OF FUN!"

Everyone won prizes, got their goody bags, and thanked each other for such a great day. The adults had just as much fun as the children, and to the surprise of the children, the adults started talking about planning the next event so that the community could come together again.

Everyone thought this was something the community should do more often.

ACTIVITIES

Connect the dots and color the picture, and write a sentence about the different items.

ACTIVITIES

Search and find all the items that was not at the party .

About the Author

Annette Wilson is the mother of four children (two boys and two girls), grandmother of one child (Victoriann), and aunt to many nieces and nephews.

Annette is a Macrobiotic/Natural Food Chef who loves sharing her cooking skills with all her young children.

I was privileged to be able to stay home, work part time, and raise my children. Although I had a hand in the upbringing of my younger siblings, having the full responsibility of raising your own is not quite the same. I was really and truly Mom, a mom who was expected to take on life's challenges and perform miracles from a child's point of view, and in many instances, I did. I learned a lot from my own children and siblings but did not realize that was only the beginning; I had a whole lot more to learn in a different environment. I had great fun with my nephew Damian; I took care of him for almost two years while his mother finished her schooling. I also had the great opportunity to care for my granddaughter for almost four years so her parents could attend university. Here again, I had to be mom and grandma, a great education indeed.

After moving to the United States, I found myself surrounded with kids from various ages, cooking for them as well as taking care of them, babysitting, and being a mom in a different setting, but a true mom.

I was privileged to work with a number of families, taking care of their little ones, as young as three months old to teens. It was a learning experience all the way. I learned that babies, toddlers, and teens have one big need: TO BE LOVED, TO BE UNDERSTOOD, TO SHOW AND BE KIND TO THEM, AND TO BE PATIENT WITH THEM. It does not matter what the culture is, they need to be loved and understood. Giving these, you automatically become the new mom in the life of the child you come to love. It doesn't matter who or what you look like; the soft touch, the love, the warm smile, the genuine care and look will keep them coming and even caring for you in return. I got a lot of that and still do. That bond was so close, I was allowed to give some of those kids pet names, like THE BOZZ, Chicken Hider, Soso, Debonzo, 10 Cents, Meme, and the list goes on.

Today, as I look at some of these beautiful, smart, well-grounded teens whom I cared for as babies, not sure that I would have a part in their adult life, I feel really good that those my hands touched are doing really well.

Love and thanks for allowing me to share a small part of your lives, so rewarding, so enriching and fulfilling.

To all these children, I really and truly love all of you. I know that you all know and appreciate it. Thanks for the surprised phone calls now and again to check in on me or just share a funny joke. Thanks for loving me back!

Printed in the United States
By Bookmasters